Living Life with Joy in My Heart

My Journey through Grief

SPIRIT: The divine essence that guides
us when our hearts are open.

Ruthann Lees

BALBOA.
PRESS

A DIVISION OF HAY HOUSE

Balboa Press books may be ordered through booksellers or by contacting:

Balboa Press
A Division of Hay House
1663 Liberty Drive
Bloomington, IN 47403
www.balboapress.com
1 (877) 407-4847

Because of the dynamic nature of the Internet, any web addresses or
links contained in this book may have changed since publication and
may no longer be valid. The views expressed in this work are solely those
of the author and do not necessarily reflect the views of the publisher,
and the publisher hereby disclaims any responsibility for them.

The author of this book does not dispense medical advice or prescribe the use
of any technique as a form of treatment for physical, emotional, or medical
problems without the advice of a physician, either directly or indirectly. The
intent of the author is only to offer information of a general nature to help
you in your quest for emotional and spiritual well-being. In the event you use
any of the information in this book for yourself, which is your constitutional
right, the author and the publisher assume no responsibility for your actions.

Quotation from the Pathwork® Guide Lecture Material © 2000 the Pathwork
Foundation. Reprinted by permission of the Pathwork Foundation."

Any people depicted in stock imagery provided by Thinkstock are models,
and such images are being used for illustrative purposes only.
Certain stock imagery © Thinkstock.

Printed in the United States of America.

ISBN: 978-1-4525-1507-6 (sc)
ISBN: 978-1-4525-1509-0 (hc)
ISBN: 978-1-4525-1508-3 (e)

Library of Congress Control Number: 2014909069

Balboa Press rev. date: 05/30/2014

Contents

Chapter 1   When I Thought My Heart Would Break..........1

Chapter 2   Knowing I Will Survive.................................17

Chapter 3   Coming through It and Finding Joy.................27

Chapter 4   Finding the Real Me....................................57

Chapter 5   Knowing Love Never Ends............................71

Books That Have Influenced My Journey..........................81

Postscript...89

With Deep Gratitude...91

Permissions..93

About the Author...95

We are both in a good place and we are very much together. This is more wonderful than what was, my dear. We are both growing now in the ways we are meant to be growing… Nothing is by accident. All is part of the plan, the master plan. You are coming into your own, the person you are meant to be. You are becoming more filled with light all of the time. Each of the things that you do help with this. You are able to focus on your goal and stay with this. Incorporating the disciplines (yoga and meditation) into your life are so helpful as is the time of writing that we do together. Know you are a beautiful light to so many. All you need you have within you, my dear. It is easy to become caught up with things in the outer. It is much more difficult to keep the focus on the inner and this truly is the test for each on earth, to come into their own perfection. This is a process and must be realized by each. Thank you for spending time and allowing me to be with you this way. My love and presence is with you always.

— Don Lees

Dear Reader,

These past years since the death of my husband Don, I have dropped to painful lows, risen to joyful highs, and soared to new levels of being. It has been a crash course from dependent to independent living. My life as a quiet, supportive wife, content and coupled, was changed forever in a moment.

Through the years, I have attended spiritual retreats and studied effective prayer, healing, personal survival, and explored mystical and paranormal experience. My studies were fulfilling and expanding, yet not as transforming as experiencing the death of one's life partner. This book is a personal milestone.

Through the practice of journaling, I dialogue with spirit. Almost mystically, Don had gifted me a journaling workshop for my birthday years before he died, but journaling has become a means for us to communicate, perhaps better and deeper than it ever was.

Don and I learned dowsing in workshops and practiced it together. I feel we are still using it.

As difficult as it is to reconcile the loss of my spouse, home remodeler and true love, I would not have experienced this soul growth if Don were still here with me in body.

Knowing we each experience loss and grief in our own time and in our own ways, I offer you my experience. It is my deep desire that you too will find your emerging butterfly.

With love and gratitude,
Ruthann Lees

Chapter One

When I Thought My Heart Would Break

A Broken Heart is An Open Heart

S uddenly one day my world fell apart. In an instant, life changed and I knew life would never be the same. All of the dreams I had visioned for what life would bring vanished. I was alone. No longer a twosome, a couple, I was suddenly alone and single again. How could I carry on without my loving husband in my life? Pain and numbness filled my body.

Sleep wouldn't come. Tired, I would fall asleep only to awaken soon afterward with jumbled thoughts racing through my mind. Then the pain in my chest made me wonder, *am I having a heart attack?* The hours of darkness were unending. When daylight finally came, I couldn't make myself get out of bed and start another day. *What's the point? Who cares if I live or die?* I really wanted to die and be with my beloved husband. Life without him seemed too hard to face.

My children and my mother were also devastated and grieving. Somehow, I realized I could not add to their already heavy burden of grief. I had to pull myself together and go on without the love of my life. For days it was an effort. Even with my family present, I could not eat, nor could I sleep through the night. When my family returned to their homes and their lives, I was alone in my big house. The bed I once shared for all those years was empty and a very lonesome place. I wanted to be held and comforted, but I was alone. The tears flowed and my weary body ached with the loneliness.

The Earthquakes Within

Exactly four weeks after my husband's physical death I became intensely aware of the anger and resentment I was feeling. I sat down as I had so many times before when filled with great emotion and began to journal asking for guidance and help. How could I release my intense feelings in a healthy and healing way, a nondestructive manner? Spirit responded quickly.

Dear, dear Ruthie, you are loved more than you can possibly realize. With Don being in spirit it doesn't mean the love from him is gone for it is as strong as before and perhaps even more so. You are realizing just how deeply you loved him. It is OK, know that what is expressed now is still felt so let it pour through you to him and on to all of the others in your life. This is the answer:

LOVE. First of all, love yourself because without that as a base there is no love to be given to others around you. Everyone needs love and especially at times of such loss, and all are feeling this loss. It is just that yours is perhaps the greatest because he was part of your daily life and living. There is no way to really replace that loss, especially at this time, but know that you will be able to find ways of coping and dealing with it. Reach out to others. Do not close them off. Do not close yourself off from the love they want and need to express. Receive it and let it help you to heal yourself. This is a good day for you to really allow yourself to just "be." Be where you are, feel what you are feeling, and release it. Spirit is with you and you will begin to feel better as feelings are released and expressed. Do not keep emotions bottled up inside because that makes a time bomb when great emotion has no outlet. Once you have started on the way to helping and healing yourself, you can continue in a more effective way to help others who are grieving this loss with you, most of all your children. They too have experienced tremendous loss. They need to continue their grief process. This is not a quick fix thing. Healing the emotional heartache will take time. You will be able to do this. Know this at the deepest levels of your being. It will one day become much better, but only as the process of grieving is allowed to progress and continue. It takes time and it takes some work. It won't just happen, especially if emotion is pushed down and not given expression. It is OK to feel anger and resentment. These are honest emotions and need to have an outlet. The anger can be expressed in positive ways that are not destructive. It is an energy and needs the release from the body. Doing something physical is a way to let it out and let it go. Release all of the powerful energy that builds up inside of you and do this in positive ways like beating a pillow or loud expression when in a safe place or movement of the body or even the crying and sobbing serve to release the power inside of you. Know and believe it will get better, but only when action is taken and the emotion is given expression. Feel the love being sent to you.

The following day my whole body was aching from the pain of my grief. In my journal I expressed how weak and fragile I felt and asked God what I might do to start feeling more strength and energy. At the same time, I was wondering if this was too soon to be wanting and asking for it. Again, Spirit responded.

Remember that you are not alone, not now, not ever. In a sense, you are being carried along and what you are experiencing is not uncommon. Do not expect so much from yourself. You have experienced probably the ultimate loss and it is hard. The emotions are very close to the surface and they give you earthquakes within. That is because of the great force and pressure of these emotions. They must be released. Let the tears flow and know that is healing for you. It is not a sign of weakness or of anything but your great sadness at the loss of your very best and closest friend in this world. He was your cheerleader, your helper, your healer, your lover, and your confidant. You told him everything and shared yourself with him. Now you are feeling cut off and alone. This was a very special relationship. You need to take special care of yourself. Don't try to do as much as you have felt like you need to be doing. When you make one step it is enough for now. You will be able to do more when you have had a chance to heal more. You have just begun this process of healing your grief. It is good you are starting to let it out of your body, it is a must for your own well being. What you are going through has affected many people. It is almost overwhelming in itself the great numbers of people who were affected and touched in very deep ways by him. He is a truly beautiful spirit and is with you. You need to know this and realize it. He is lending his support to you even now and will continue to do this as long as you need it. He wants you to know that he is with you and trying hard to comfort you and wants you to know that all is well with him.

A Message from Beyond

Every night while I lay in bed trying to fall asleep I would experience a strange sensation across my shoulders and neck. This feeling was hard to describe and persisted even though I placed a pillow against my back creating the illusion that I was not alone. It was a prickly feeling, and it persisted. This continued until I discovered the probable cause.

A board meeting for Spiritual Frontiers Fellowship International was scheduled in Philadelphia one month after Don's physical death. Being a member of this board, I decided to attend despite friends' reservations that this activity was too much, too soon, but I wanted to be there.

While packing for this trip, I went to get my special neck pillow from the bedside cabinet. The door to the cabinet was closed. I couldn't believe it! Several weeks before, Don said the magnetic mechanism which held the door in place didn't work, and there was no way I was going to get the door to stay shut, because he had tried. So the door hung open at a 45 degree angle. But this day, it was tightly closed! I stood there in utter amazement trying to figure it out. Nobody had been in my bedroom except me. I phoned my son who in the previous week had spent a couple of days helping me with several necessary tasks. Because this task had not been on my mind during his visit, I had to know if for some reason he had come into my bedroom and fixed the latch. He had not. Both of us were mystified until we realized it was Don's way of letting us know he was still with us. After all, he was an engineer and throughout his earthly life loved challenges, remodeling, and fixing things for me was one of his greatest delights. This is what he always had done. What better way could there be to let me know he was still here.

While I was in Philadelphia attending the Spiritual Frontiers Fellowship Board meeting, two gifted and loving friends offered me assistance. I discovered from one of my fellow board members that the spirit of Don was staying very close to me in an effort to comfort me. This friend sees and communicates with spirits. She asked him to give me my space, then told me that he was learning how to be "in spirit" as much as I was learning to carry on alone.

Another friend offered me a Reiki energy treatment. After we had all gone out to eat and shortly before going to bed, I received an incredible healing from my friend who is a 3rd level Reiki Master. Wondrously and peacefully, I slept for eight hours straight. This was the first time I had experienced uninterrupted sleep in a month. My appetite improved, and amazingly, the "prickles" on my back and neck disappeared as Don learned about my need for breathing room.

Recognizing Our Preparation

About seven months before these life changing events, Don and I had gone to a workshop in Kansas City to hear Dannion Brinkley talk about being *Saved by the Light: My Near Death Experience* and Robert Grant's presentation on *Dimensions of Death and Dying*. Both of us had been reading and learning about these topics over the previous year.

I found statements among the notes Don had taken at that conference to support the continuance of consciousness, that there is no death. His notes read:

The more we take thought of the NDE's (near death experiences) etc., the more we are ready for the process of death ourselves. The thing we came to earth to do is love everyone. The church and physicians years ago changed the belief system to one of "If we can not see it, it is not real." These changes occurred and we still hold on to them. "We are in a little physical box passing through time and space— this is as dead as it gets, folks!" We have to narrow from 10,000 to 3 dimensions when we come into a physical body. If there was an original sin, it is that we forgot our union with God.

When Don suddenly collapsed as we were starting our evening walk, I remember thinking he would come back and tell me what his NDE was like. Having shared these NDE interests, I couldn't believe and did not want to accept the finality of his sudden physical death. How could this be happening? Why was this happening to me, to us? How does one go on without the love of their life?

The pain of my grief at times felt unbearable. Two months later, I wrote in my journal when I awakened early with unsettled feelings. I had gotten up to meditate and began to feel very sad so I sat and wrote to let go of my pain. From experience, this is a way to let my tears begin to flow. *Oh Don, I'm missing you so much. I want you to hold me, to kiss me, to tell me you love me, and that all is well.* It was time for more of my sadness and grief to come out. The tears flowed and I couldn't breathe. My heart and my back ached. It was good to let it come, to feel it, and to not ignore or close it off. As I wrote, Don spoke to me.

Thank you, my dear. I am here and I understand your sadness. Don't worry about me. I want to be with you. You know how much I love you and have for so long now. It isn't easy for me to leave you. I am glad I can stand by you this way and continue to tell you of my love and feelings for you. You know it was hard for us to talk about this when we were together. This may work better for me where I can transfer my thoughts to you on paper. It is really good you learned to do this for now we can continue to be in contact. I can talk to you and tell you that my love for you is still very much with you.

You helped me in so many ways while we shared our life together. Know that. Believe it. It is true. How could I have learned about life in spirit if it weren't for you. Remember all the reading you did to me as we traveled? Well, while I wasn't very much interested in reading myself, I was interested in learning more and you did that for me. I want you to know how helpful this has been for me to know more and be at a better place here on this side. It is a good place to be, so free, so light, so happy. I want you to know that I am in a good place and I will continue to be with you and cheering you on. You are a light and it does shine brightly. I can see it and I want you to be fully aware of it my dear.

Thank you for letting me tell you these things. It is important to me to continue to be in contact with you and to help you through this time of change in your life. It is going to be O. K. You have a purpose to fulfill and you will do very well. You will be helping a lot of people in the future. Know that this is all part of the bigger plan. All is in order and all will work out. Don't be in too big of a hurry for the next step. This is a time for healing— a time for being— not doing.

Through a series of unusual events, I found Don very much with me. In fact, in this limitless form without a physical body, he was able to be present with me, with our daughter, our son, his mother, and perhaps a host of others all at the same time.

I found out just how much I had been limiting spirit after it leaves the physical body, forgetting the multidimensional aspects of spirit. Oh, how limiting my thoughts and beliefs could be.

Living the Loss

I began attending a Bereavement Support group at my church led by Joy and Marvin Johnson, professionals in bereavement work. When I found myself in difficulty the morning after my first group meeting, I thought of Joy. I had taken the trash, yard waste, and recyclables to the curb. Suddenly, my heart was pounding, I was lightheaded, short of breath, nauseated, and weak. I went into the house and sat down.

Not wanting to go to the emergency room, I called Joy. She thought it sounded as if I was having an anxiety attack and suggested doing a grounding meditation. I sat in a chair with another chair facing me. I visualized Don in that chair and extended my hands as though we were holding hands. With both feet flat on the floor and my eyes closed, I told him what I was feeling. I did some deep breathing in and out while counting down from ten. I found myself relaxing and starting to feel much better.

Later that day, Joy called to see how I was doing. She had seen Don in front of her, telling her I had gotten into an energy trail (something she had not heard of before). This made sense to me as I had used his two wheel dolly to take the bag of newspapers to the curb. This was the first time I had put my hands on it and I realized immediately that it was carrying his energy. My hand on the dolly was a hand on Don.

I discovered how hard the holidays and special days like birthdays could be. Each one of the "firsts" proved to be difficult experiences. Thanksgiving came less than two months after Don's death. Living in the same city with many of Don's family members meant that throughout our marriage, family gatherings were part of our holiday celebrations. Since my mother had been widowed for all but two of the 36 years of my marriage and I am her only family living near by, she has been included.

Going to our niece's home for this Thanksgiving Dinner was particularly painful for me. Being totally consumed with my feelings of loss, I wanted others to talk to me about him. It seemed as if no one would. I couldn't find the words to ask them to tell me their memories of him. I felt so alone and was in such pain grieving my loss that although I was surrounded by a family who loved me, I was not able to open up enough to fully receive their love. When dinner came to a close, I found out that family at the other table had been remembering and talking about Don. I left with my heart aching, thinking that I sat at the wrong table, and wishing I had heard their stories.

Days drug by. Christmas came. My most difficult moment was during the Christmas Eve service when all were holding lighted candles and singing "Silent Night." Memories of Christmas Eve services with Don began to flood my mind and tears filled my eyes. I felt alone while being surrounded by people. That night I had a hard time sleeping. Waking up in the middle of the night, I picked up my journal. I was feeling Don's presence and I began to write.

I want to tell you how very much your love means to me and let you know my love is still with you. You are so important to so many people. You need to know this, they are so wanting to help you and to do for you. Be loving to them and appreciative of their efforts. This will be a good day. It will be filled with many surprises and happy things for you. Be open to receive and enjoy all of it. Yes, it is good to let those tears flow, but only for short periods. This is a time to celebrate and be filled with joy. The love is born within you and needs to be expressed fully to others. Let it just flow forth. My love is with you now and always…. Focus on external things, the people around you. Let the emotion and thoughts be directed in that way. Thank you for letting me express to you these things and being open to spirit and the guidance you can receive if you are open to it. Life is wonderful, enjoy it, live it, and be happy, my dear. You are loved, you are important, and you can do it. This is the time to be fully present to those who love you.

I am so thankful for an opportunity to let you know these things. I love you and I am with you. You would be surprised to know how much can be accomplished from this side, so relax, my honey, and let it happen. It will and it will be good. You will be happy. You will have a good life. It will be good—wait and see. Trust me.

I put the journal down and turned on the TV. It was 3 A.M. The movie "Always" with Richard Dreyfus was on the screen. It touched me where I needed to be touched. I cried the tears that were needing to be released. Dreyfus, who is in spirit, is trying desperately to make his wife hear him. "The love we hold back is the only pain we have," he tells his wife toward the end of the movie. I grabbed my journal again and wrote a message to myself to give my love freely to all in my life beginning today— Christmas Day.

Freeing Love and Gratitude

The following day I read from a Unity booklet, *The Promise of Christmas*. "Today, the first day of Christmas, I grow in Faith. In faith I start a new life, I make new decisions and I establish new goals." How right on target for me, especially now. Then Spirit confirmed this for me.

So relax, be at peace, be joy filled for all is well and all is definitely working for good. It is time to be an observer and watch it unfold. You will see that it will happen and in some surprising and amazing ways, so just enjoy the happenings as they come to you. Yes, it is in faith this must be done.

My birthday came exactly one month later. Knowing this would be a difficult time, my son, daughter-in-law, and my mother came to spend the weekend with me. I rose early that day and wrote in my journal. "Yes, this is my 62nd birthday and I am most grateful to have Jeff, Melanie, and Mom here with me to celebrate my day. It has been a while since I've given you a chance to write to me, my honey. Would you like to do that?"

Of course, I want to say hello to you and to tell you that I love you and I am here with you, so very close to you. You are so very important and special to me, my dear. I can never tell you how very much you mean to me and to so many people. It is immeasurable. You must know it and believe it deep within. It is important that you keep on loving all of those near and dear to you as you have, only be sure to tell them and let them know of your deep love for them. Keep that love flowing out from you, out from within you, out to all. It is what is important. I know now how important that is and I wish I had been able to tell you in the ways I always felt how much I love you. It is very deep and very strong and has been for such a long time. Time is not important on this side, so that is hard to measure. Please be sure that you tell Jeff, Melanie, your Mom, and all of the family of my love for them as well. I am aware of so much now and know this is of great importance. Love is what it is all about. The great accepting and nonjudgmental kind of love. All need this. You are there and you can do this. You can show it and express it many ways. Keep passing it on. Know I am with you, my dear, and enjoy this special day of yours.

This was a wonderful gift to receive on my birthday and I was reminded to express my deep love and gratitude to my family everyday. I was needing to be encouraged to do this. It seems that I probably still need reminders from time to time. Although with practice and time, remembering to tell others of my love and appreciation for them becomes easier. There is no question about how much happier this makes me feel.

It was on this birthday that Jeff and Melanie gave me a wonderful gift by installing a modem on my computer connecting me to the world of emailing. Just a few months later, I realized how truly incredible this gift was as I began receiving emails from my son as he traveled around the world. Instantly, I heard about his experiences in Barranquilla, Columbia in South America, Sydney, Australia, and London as he traveled for his consulting job to each of these countries. I also began emailing others and my world, which had felt so empty and alone, began changing. This gift changed my life by expanding my world, putting me in close touch with many people. It was amazing to find how many of my friends and family were already connected to cyberspace.

Another Reminder

On Easter weekend, a mysterious thing happened. My mother and I were in my family room watching a video and had been talking about Don that Saturday night. At a particularly intense point in the film, Don's picture flew off the shelf above the TV and onto the floor. We looked at each other questioning how this happened. The 4" x 5" framed picture had been at least an inch away from the edge of the shelf. Was this Don letting us know he was right there with us? We could not come up with any other explanation. The doors and windows were closed so there was no wind. We had not felt any strong vibrations. A week after this happened while dialoguing with Don in my journal, I wrote:

Yes, I am with you much of the time and I want you to know this and be aware of it. How much better way to show you this than with the energy move of my picture.

When Don's birthday came six months after his transition, I decided to make it an occasion for remembering him. Knowing this would also be a difficult time for his mother and sister, I invited them along with my brother-in-law to a special dinner at our favorite Chinese restaurant. It was a place the two of us had often taken his mother for dinner. The four of us had an evening filled with sharing memories of Don and it was good. We did indeed remember and celebrate his life. This proved to be a healing time for all of us as we supported each other in remembering his special day.

Looking back I realize how much I accomplished during those six months. There was a great deal of help from others, and I believe, with Don's guidance. Financial decisions were slowly made one by one. Taking "baby steps" throughout was the only way I could proceed. My healing was underway and I was beginning to be aware of my progress, yet little did I realize the vast mysterious journey still ahead of me. And Spirit spoke to me.

Unless mystery is a part of your life, I am not a part of your life, for I am mystery.

Chapter Two

Knowing I Will Survive

I am filled with Light and Love.

After several months when I came to the realization that I did indeed have reasons to live, my life changed once again. I knew that I wanted to help others who had experienced loss as I had and to let them know that life does not end. There is life beyond the shedding of the body that we inhabit while we are here. Consciousness does indeed survive bodily death. It is a transition to another way of being without a physical body, a transition to spirit.

Unexpected Confirmation

While I had been at a Spiritual Frontiers Fellowship annual conference, I had been told in a spiritual counseling session that my beloved Don was wanting to sing to me and I needed to listen. This amused me a great deal because we had laughed together about his love of singing, especially the hymns at church even though he might not always sing the right notes or be in the right key. This never intimidated him. He always sang out with great joy.

A week later, while I was in the shower, a song came to me. Spontaneously I was singing unfamiliar words to a beautiful melody. The words and melody were truly an inspired gift. As soon as I was out of the shower, I ran to find pen and paper so I could write them down, knowing these inspirations often vanish like a dream. This is what I had sung so unexpectedly and melodiously:

HIS SONG TO HER

Listen to my song, he said
Listen to my song
Listen to my song, he said
You will understand.
I had something else to do
Had to move along
I had something else to do
It was in the Plan.
Long ago we made this plan
Do you now recall?
Long ago we made this plan
Have to carry on.
I am with you now, you see.

I am with you still.

I am with you now, you see

Couldn't leave your heart.

We will still be here for you

We will still be here

We are with you always, dear.

Love will keep us close.

Listen to my song, he said.

Listen to my song.

Listen to my song, he said

Now you understand.

This was the confirmation I was needing.

Unveiling an Unconscious Intention

At a workshop several months into my grief, participants were working on *Dowsing Our Soul's Purpose.* I was devastated when I dowsed that I had no will to live. This came as a big shock to me as I thought I had already worked through this. Consciously I was wanting to help others, but subconsciously I was not wanting to be here. This meant that my body might find a way to help me out of this lifetime and it shook me to my core. I sobbed uncontrollably.

I knew I could carry on, because I was not alone. I had help. Lots of help. All I had to do was recognize this and *ASK* for the help I needed. From that point on, I knew beyond any doubt that we in the physical are assisted by spirit. Asking is the key word to remember. Someone once said, *"A stands for Ask, S for Seek, and K for Knock."* Like Jesus said, *"Ask, and it will be given you; seek, and you will find; knock and it will be opened to you."*

My willingness to ask is slowly changing me. Many of my old habits are being recognized and transformed. For example, parts of an old pattern are my bulldozing full steam ahead, doing things by myself in my own way, and thinking my way is best. Within this process I am observing myself, I see what more is possible, and I am becoming a different person.

As I change, I find the help needed is available. The sudden loss of Don threatened my very existence, but it also brought to my awareness fears of being out of control and needing to be in control. This transformational process is about my releasing the need for control, or said another way, a surrendering of self and of ego. However, I could not do this alone. It feels good to know that I truly am not alone. All I need to do is prayerfully ask for guidance, to be still, and listen. The still small voice is there.

Guidance is Present

Guidance comes in a number of ways. It comes through something said by a friend, something I've read, or from a dream. Often inspiration appears slowly encouraging me to take a particular action to resolve an issue. Sometimes inspiration happens very quickly and I respond, but full resolution may take a lot longer. Although I have questioned the information from time to time, I have applied it. This has required that I learn to trust that what I need to know will come to me at the right time, but sometimes patience is a necessary quality.

Much of my guidance has come in the form of dialoguing with Don's spirit through journaling. I had learned to dialogue with spirit at an *Ira Progoff Journal Workshop* held at our church. I look back at that time now with a lot of gratitude for I found it both helpful and very easy for me to do. It set the stage for my growth and understanding in continuity of consciousness.

My journal documented a time following another SFFI Board meeting, the second one I attended following Don's transition. This was my first attempt at journaling by computer where I noted that the days and weeks were disappearing quickly. It felt like a time to be in touch with Don so I was open to receive his thoughts.

Thank you for letting me come through. This way I know that we are communicating and that you can go back and refer to the words that are on paper and not just rely on the thoughts I send. Let it flow and do not think as you let your fingers move over the keyboard. I am so happy with all that you are doing in your progress with the taxes and all. You did an excellent job and were able to turn it in before your trip. It was fun to be in Washington. I enjoyed that time with you and I know you were remembering the time we were there together. So happy you are able to do these things and be with people that understand and are so very helpful to you. The work you are doing at church is very good. (The issue of death and dying) is something we both were hoping to have the church address and you must know that you are an important part of how that is coming together. I am so pleased to see how much more open you are in expressing what you know. It is why you are where you are and so continue to do this work. It needs to be known by more people. It is time for many more to be enlightened and aware of the continuation of life. It does not end.

At the close of that day of dialogue, I asked if there were some other things he would like to say to me.

Here is the area that needs work on a regular daily basis. Keep with the disciplines of meditation and staying clear and open to spirit. Keep asking spirit for guidance. Ask and you will receive. You know this well, but sometimes it is not the way you operate, so remember it is the way and keep practicing. I am telling you this as a reminder and in love. When you ask spirit to give the answers you know that all flows in divine order for you.

My Personal Forms of Healing

At the time I was told by a friend to listen to Don's songs, I was also told that he is now one of my guides, working with me. This was truly affirming. I knew of his presence, but I was unaware of him being my guide and I really liked the idea. It seemed quite natural for Don to be a guide because I had depended on him throughout our 36 years of marriage. Consequently, I felt compelled to communicate more deeply with him, and he responded.

I do love you so very much and I am here with you. You have to believe this and know it in your innermost being. I am happy that you had confirmation and can perhaps start to really know and believe that I am and will be with you. We have work to do together and know that this will be fun for you. You developed the ability to do this years ago and now it is time we do this on a regular basis so the work can develop. Practice will help. I know you know that! There are many things to reveal to you this way and it is important that we start to do this on a regular basis. I am hoping you will spend more time asking questions mentally so I can give you assistance in thought. You have been told many times that you are clairvoyant. Believe and trust in this process. We must be about doing it and make it a priority. This will take some discipline on your part as you seem to stay busy. I can help you so much more from this side than I was able to when I was with you in body. I know this now. The picture is so much bigger and broader from where I am. Know that what you are to be doing and to be about is beginning now in this time. It will be an exciting adventure and we are creating this together. Let's take this a step at a time and know that it will unfold before you. We are a team, my dear, and I can help you in many more ways. I am here for you and know it is not an easy adjustment, so do not be hard on yourself and allow the tears to flow when they come. It is healing. Most of the time you carry on with your life and are functioning very well. Just let your feelings flow and know this is important to do when you are in body. Recognize feelings, express them, and do not hold them buried within you. (At this point my tears were flowing.) The tears are good. They are helpful to you. It is important to also show this to others. They will learn as much from your example as from your words. So learn to let it all hang out. Have fun, laugh and be happy, too. There is a time for both. Remember this. It is a balance. Relax and don't feel you have to be so in control of your emotions and what you are feeling. Express them. I know this is something you can do, my dear. This will be of help to others, too.

When I wrote these words they flowed rapidly from my fingers, faster than I could have expressed them. It was such a healing process for me. I share them with the hope that they will be helpful and meaningful. As all these words come through me, I continue to be in awe of this process. **Journaling** is a form of healing for me.

Healing comes to us in many ways and certainly not all at once. It takes time. Some people may think when x number of weeks has gone by you should be over the loss and ready to move on with your life. Contrary to this, the length of time for healing varies and depends on many factors.

I never really know when the tears are going to surface or what might trigger the sense of loss I feel. For example, the tears "came out of the blue" while I was getting ready to attend a 40th anniversary party for Don's sister and her husband. I didn't immediately recognize my feelings, but later I identified a specific loss as sorrow over not having had the opportunity to share that many years with Don. I felt so alone at this event, and at the same time, I knew it would have been most meaningful for him. All of these events hold such precious memories, especially our wedding anniversary when I revisit my grief. The possibility of grieving is always present, but the stimulation of deep sadness from such events happens less frequently now.

The **sharing of memories** has been a form of my healing. I became so aware of this when the minister visited with our family to plan the memorial service to celebrate Don's life. He suggested each of us share our memories by starting with Don's sister who had known him the longest and ending with our son who was the youngest. There seemed to be an immediate shift among us even though we were very much in shock from the sudden loss. When we realized how greatly this helped us, we incorporated a time of sharing in the memorial service. From that time on, I have been aware of how beneficial it is to share these stories about my beloved and how he affected the lives of those he had touched.

Another way I find to heal is by **being with those who experience loss**. It is an opportunity to be present with another and hear them express their feelings of loss and grief. This somehow helps both of us to heal, to become more whole. As I am able to let others share their pain and grief openly, they have permission to release their feelings. From a greater perspective, we take the opportunity to recognize our common human suffering. Our words become less important as our listening ears and understanding hearts take precedence.

Chapter Three

Coming through It and Finding Joy

My Joy is My Sorrow Unmasked.

M any years ago I was told I would be teaching others how to live. In preparation, I was to understand death and dying as a necessary step in learning how to live. These words mystified me. I had experienced the death of my grandparents prior to my marriage followed by the loss of my father when I was a young wife and mother. All of these losses had occurred early in my life. Although I knew about hospice and had read a couple of books on the subject of death and dying, *how could I begin to do this?* My best friend became interested and took training in hospice. I was not motivated to do this.

Life for me had always revolved around family. After my grown daughter and son left home, my focus shifted to Don and our relationship. Soon after our son graduated from college and began life on his own, Don left the company he had been with for 25 years. Financial circumstances in our life drastically changed and it became necessary for me to re-enter the work world.

Our financial demands required that I draw an income until Don found a position in his field of expertise. While working, I regained an independence I had slowly relinquished through the years, and like Don, I began to enjoy this work life. In addition to finding work fulfilling and rewarding, we became able during our leisure time to help others as mentors. We had feelings of satisfaction but it seemed as though something often happened to interfere with my sense of joy.

At that time in my life, I was not focusing on joy. Life was serious business. It was important for me to be perfect and to please others who would then accept me and love me *more*.

An Awareness of Interference

Spirit had been guiding me in my journaling sessions to become balanced and clear. For more than a year, I had been attending a variety of workshops and conferences in order to reach the goal of writing my story. As it happened, a friend told me about a medical intuitive who had come to town to give private counseling sessions. I *knew* it was important for me to see her. This is how I became aware of emotional blocks that were interfering with my healing progress.

Through this medical intuitive, I discovered that I came into this world thinking I had to please in order to be accepted and loved. While I was in utero, my mother had deep reservations about having another baby. My parents had very little income, lived in a small apartment, and already had a 6 year old boy. My mother's thoughts imprinted my emotional body and for six decades I lived to please all the significant people in my life, especially my mother (except perhaps for those self-absorbed teen years).

I was shocked by the idea of an imprint of my mother not wanting this pregnancy. She has always told me of her delight in having a daughter when I was born. And I experienced conflict with my mother for much of my life. We have done a lot of clearing and forgiveness work as a result of my mother having studied *A Course In Miracles* for several years. She became as eager as I to have a better relationship, which took a "180 degree turn" several years ago after having cried together and asked for each other's forgiveness. So this discovery through the medical intuitive that I still had a mother issue came as a big surprise to me, because I thought I had done that from A to Z through the 18 years of working with it. What this piece of information told me was why and how I was unable to recognize joy in my relationship with my mother. For all these years, my focus was on pleasing everyone, except myself. Deep issues have taken a long time to surface and come into my awareness.

We celebrated my mother's 97th birthday with several gatherings throughout the month so all family members could participate. It is a gift to have this extended time together to celebrate our joy for each other!

A New Way of Being

Knowing and experiencing JOY is becoming more real in my life. My awareness of the circle of loved ones who are with me in spirit demonstrates that I am not alone even though it might appear otherwise. Guidance and help is readily available when I ask for it. This has perhaps been one of the hardest things for me to learn as it means relinquishing control of my life. It is a surrendering to and trusting in my inner guidance. Through this process I am discovering a new way of being. It is a way that brings greater ease in living life.

A number of experiences have brought me to this place. A year and a half after Don's transition I was awakened in the early morning by a voice that called my name. I began to write.

What is a death? It is a loss of something in your life. It is not a bad thing to have happen. It can be good and helpful to one. When something dies, something new is born to take it's place. There are many kinds of death. There are deaths of people and there are deaths of parts of self. You have experienced this loss many times and always something has been given to you to replace the loss. Something new is born or brought into your life. Remember and learn to rejoice as this is growth for you as a soul. Create a ritual which will make this a memorable time. You are dying to what has been in your life and at the same time being born into something new, a new you, a new way of being. This is the same as what I have experienced and it is good. It is to be celebrated. Rejoice in your new life, in your new way of being. Feel the joy as I do and be at peace. Be at one with me, be at one with all things. Recognize this day as a day of new beginnings and let your heart be filled with joy and happiness. Believe that all you need is provided for you. You are a faithful child of God and God is well pleased. Be at peace, my dear.

Relaxing, being at peace, and spending more time enjoying life, living it to the fullest possible extent are now my goals. Spending time in nature, slowing down, simply watching the birds, and listening to their joyous songs seems to turn everything around and are delightful ways to learn about the rhythm of life.

Signs and Symbols

It seems to me birds can be symbols bringing messages to us. It's my understanding that in many cultures the crow is considered a powerful sign. One day a flock of crows flew across my viewing deck in front of the sliding glass doors. They were so close and there were so many. This never occurred before nor has it since. This was a sign of change in my life, to step beyond my usual ways of viewing reality, look into my inner realms, and shift to a new way of seeing myself and the world around me. Crows, which I never used to like, have now become my friends and when they do appear on my path they simply serve as a reminder. They come at times when I'm needing the message.

A way in which I have been helped is by learning to recognize symbols and spending time in understanding their importance. I receive symbols in dreams which serve as messages. I am also given signs and symbols throughout the day. Years back I had acquired a number of dream books with lists of symbols, but had never related any of these to the awake state. Then, as often happens, Denise Linn's, *The Secret Language of Signs: How to Interpret the Coincidences and Symbols In Your Life*, appeared right in front of me. This was a message from spirit to become familiar with symbols and their meanings.

Symbols are messages with meanings that are specific to an individual. I've needed to recognize intuitively the real meaning for me. My conscious mind may not know the answer, so I reach into my unconscious mind and ask what this might mean if I did know it consciously. It is quite amazing how effective this process can be. Similarly, by concentrating on a list of symbols several possibilities emerge and I might recognize which symbol and message is meant for me. It can be an "Aha" moment.

It is my sense that humanity is at a time when it is important to once again rely on the messages given to us by spirit through signs and symbols. Over the ages, the significance of inner wisdom has lessened and been forgotten. The signs of the twenty-first century show accelerated change and are a call to recognize how symbols can help. The universe provides information, and that information directs me to live harmoniously with one another, with myself, and with the planet. I can learn to live with greater ease and experience the joy that comes with this.

Listening to Spirit

Developing inner wisdom or guidance is of great importance. It's my radar telling me the best possible decisions and bringing the highest and greatest good to me and those around me. I always ask if this is for the highest good of all. If it is, it is also for my highest good. When trusting the divine spirit within, life begins to flow with greater ease. Stepping "out of ego" is a necessary aspect of doing this successfully and takes concentrated practice. The following comparison, which a friend e-mailed me, reveals when you are acting from ego or from the spirit within:

Lesser Mind The Voice of Ego Personality Level	Greater Mind The Voice of Spirit Soul Level
Flatters	Informs
Commands	Suggests
Demands	Guides
Tests	Nudges
Chooses for you	Leaves choice to you
Imprisons	Empowers
Promotes dependency	Promotes independence
Intrudes	Respects
Pushes	Supports
Excludes	Includes
Is status oriented	Is free and open
Insists on obedience	Encourages growth
Often claims	and development
ultimate authority	Recognizes a greater
Offers short cuts	power, or God
Seeks personal gratification	Offers integration
	Affirm divine order along
	with the good of the whole

When my conscious spiritual journey began about 20 years ago, I began seeking *something more* in my life and knew I was on a spiritual path. Up to this point, my life had been filled with schooling, pursuit of a career followed by marriage, becoming a mother, and raising my children. As the children's' needs for my time and attention became less and less, I realized an emptiness in my life. Being a mother was probably one of my favorite roles as a woman but *now what was I going to do?* I had given up a career as a dietitian to become a mother and had no desire to return to it. After years of Brownies, Cubs, PTA, swim meets, ball games, and other activities, I began my search for some kind of personal fulfillment.

Somewhere along the way my involvement at church, a Methodist church, became increasingly important. Don and I became actively involved, taking various Bible studies which meant taking weekly classes in the evenings, working on committees, and helping out wherever we could. Although sporadic, prayer and meditation became a part of my daily life. My interest in prayer and meditation began my journey to self-fulfillment. I was extended an invitation to join a group of mostly younger women who had started a prayer group. This appealed to me and I joined the Becomer's Prayer Group. As we shared our personal concerns and lives praying for each other and studying a variety of topics, we became close friends.

My interest in holistic health and healing blossomed at this time. There was a fascinating big world out there with a lot of mysterious and wonderful things happening. I read one book which led to the next and my collection of books grew. My interest in spiritual teachings heightened and it was about this time that I first attended a Spiritual Frontiers Fellowship retreat. Here I pursued many exciting topics, met interesting speakers, and participated in intriguing workshops.

Nowhere else had I ever experienced such a loving environment as at these week-long retreats. The feeling of acceptance among this group of about 500 people was incredible. This was my first experience where everything seemed to happen in the right sequence and at the right time. I wanted my life to be this way.

Living the Love I Am

Learning to love unconditionally, as Jesus taught, became my goal in life. It became my mission and my passion. At a conference in 1984, I was privileged to hear Dr. Jerry Jampolsky, author of *Love is Letting Go Of Fear* and *Teach Only Love*. Hearing him speak about the principles in these books and his Attitudinal Healing Center in Tiburon, California, reinforced my growing belief in the unique and great transforming power of love. I wanted this kind of love in my life, to be able to give and receive it.

My guiding light is to learn all I can about love and to incorporate the lessons in my life, in all that I do, and in all of my relationships. It is a tall order and it has led me on an incredible journey, albeit a challenging one. This means learning to love absolutely everyone without conditions. People who appear to be the most unlovable are often the ones who are most in need of love. Being loved is a universal need and there are no exceptions.

I know we are here to love each other. It is simple, and paradoxically, it is difficult to do. From my experiences, I have had to become aware of the need for love and be able to open to receive the love which comes to me, for when I am filled with love, it becomes easier to give it to others.

My greatest need is to learn how to love myself, to know I am worthy of love, and to believe this with all my heart and soul. There are times I easily forget that each individual is a spark of the divine. Then I remember that there is no separation from the divine. Therefore, I am worthy. As for many, my worthiness is recognizable if my experiences are loving and my emotions ring true that I am lovable.

It's impossible for me to give love when I don't feel loved. It is like a well that has run dry. There simply is nothing there to give to others. Why did Jesus in his great commandment say to love others *as yourself?* Is it not then of first and greatest importance to learn to love yourself? If so, then how can this be done?

First, I know we are all magnificent and creative beings. Second, we are also spirit and come from the same source. Although our bodies demonstrate our individual differences, we are more than our bodies. Third, I see us as incredible beings who have been gifted with a variety of talents and abilities.

We are an important link to our Creator with gifts within us to be shared. Each one of us has great worth and treasures within that need to be given to the world, to bring creation to its wholeness.

All too often, these gifts become buried and forgotten. Circumstances may lead us in very different directions than those originally intended with our entry into this world. For example, I became caught up in listening to others rather than to my inner voice, and I forgot the real me. But I was nudged by all the help around me and I knew it was important to spend time in self-discovery. I had to recover a sense of who I am and what it is that I came here to do. Each day I am closer, because when a feeling of happiness comes from what I am doing, I know I am on target.

My Philosophy for Living

Life is not meant to be a struggle. It is meant to be lived with purpose and with joy in the living of it. I am here to learn as much as possible about love. This love is universal love. It is an energy, a divine energy of my very being. It is a divine energy of the universe, a spark within me, surrounding me, and found throughout all of creation. To know and realize this is essential. Without recognition of it, a connection is lost, and I am less for it, possibly resulting in not realizing my full potential.

I speak of this divine energy as God. It is also known as Universal Intelligence, Goddess, All That Is, and in more recent years, The Force. There are many names for God. I use what is most meaningful for me. The point here is that divine energy is a part of everyone and everything. It is something found outside of me, it is also within me.

When I understood that I have this divine spark within me, I realized an interconnection with everyone and with all things. Then, the Golden Rule of *doing unto others as you would have them do unto you* had renewed meaning for me. It is no mystery that versions of the golden rule appear in most religions throughout the world.

A Change of Perspective

I have observed and experienced great changes in our world. Humanity is moving toward a world that honors human worth, dignity, equality, and justice. I have great interest in finding new ways of living, ways that recognize what each one of us has in common with all of humanity, and ways of opening our hearts to the world.

In order to do this, I have had to let go of fears and start living in more loving ways. This loving and nurturing of myself fills me with a love and kindness I want to express to others. When I have found that place of love in my actions toward others, others respond in more accepting and loving ways toward me. Thus, I begin receiving as I am giving. The by-product is a life filled with more happiness and joy than I have ever known.

I have discovered that by living my life this way everything becomes better. It's like a spiral moving upward bringing me increasing amounts of joy, spreading and multiplying in all directions. What fun this is, it just keeps escalating! I find an increase in enthusiasm for life. I look forward to each day, knowing I can and will meet the challenges that come. These are opportunities given for growing and learning about my *self.* Accepting this was a change of perspective for me.

When I look back now to the time before I became a widow, I see how much I have grown and learned. Perhaps the greatest change I recognize is in my feelings of adequacy. Although others did not see me the way I saw myself, at that time I felt very inadequate. I don't know where that feeling came from, but for as long as I can remember, it plagued me. I didn't know how to overcome it. Today it is gone. I know I am adequate and can take care of myself. I am now more confident in my ability to respond and handle things as they come along. Consequently, I have become very aware of how dependent I had become on my husband to take care of me.

Although Don tried hard to help me become more independent, his direction and approval had become a way of life and very comfortable for me. In hindsight, it is easy to see the ways in which he was helping me to become self-sufficient. When the opportunity came for me to serve on the SFFI national board, I believe he saw this as a way for me to become more independent, and he readily supported my participation. My making all of the travel arrangements to attend the quarterly meetings was part of our agreement from the beginning. I became accustomed to traveling alone to these meetings and for this I am grateful. When I became a widow, it was easier for me to venture forth and travel alone.

Another change has become apparent. It is the birth of a more adventuresome spirit in the way I am choosing to live my life. When the opportunity to ride in a hot air balloon came, I excitedly accepted and did it. This surprised my family. I am more eager to experience life fully and take advantage of each opportunity as it comes along. In fact, I am more intentional about this. This new perspective opened me to the greatest change of all. I am much more willing to share my thoughts and ideas with others. I believe this opening up, finding my voice, and expressing myself is revealing who I am truly meant to be.

My Life Line

So much of my life has been spent sitting back and letting others express themselves while I watched and listened. Perhaps I learned early in my life that what I had to say was not well accepted, so I decided to keep quiet, or maybe it has been part of my nature, living more within myself. More recently, I have learned just how important it is to share my thoughts with others. In this way, a link is formed with other individuals that would not have been experienced.

I am finding that these links bring me into deep heart connections with others and enrich my life. This feeds my soul, nourishes my spirit, and in the end, brings great joy into my life. It has become my lifeline. The diversity of experience and information, which is now openly shared, enriches me. It makes my journey easier by lightening the load, because whole new worlds are opening before me. Sharing in the discovery is more fun than trying to go it alone. My life line is that I really do need others and I need to experience community from this heart space.

Being in community at this deeper level adds to my life. No individual has all of the answers or solutions to life's challenges, so by the sharing and pooling of information, lives are enriched. Sometimes just hearing myself verbalize my thoughts brings the answers I am seeking and likewise stimulates a new perspective for another. Inspirations, which come from spirit, become accessible when spoken. It is as if God calls for people to awaken each other.

Essentially, it is about listening. The answers to my questions are already within me. It has become my task to recognize that this is possible, to learn to listen, and to hear the information given. But there is a caution and that requires me to exercise discernment. Is the information coming from my ego or is it coming from Spirit? Stepping out of ego and allowing the pure message to come from Spirit is always important in this process.

For me to hear Spirit, I am challenged by living with fear or living with love. Recognizing and letting go of fear is a major challenge. There are many fears that I have experienced. A few years ago, I heard an excellent definition of fear. FEAR is **F**alse **E**vidence **A**ppearing **R**eal. In other words, fears are in our thoughts, but thoughts can be transformed. Thoughts of fear can be replaced with thoughts of love. It takes effort to do this, but it is certainly well worth the time required.

Asking God to help is a good way to begin this transformation process. Never underestimate the power of asking for help. Many of us have laboriously worked on this in a variety of ways, however, we are now in a time when this transformation can occur much more rapidly. First, it takes awareness that a change is necessary. Second, there must be a desire to bring about the change. Third, the asking is done with intention. Finally, prepare for miracles as they will most definitely occur.

Pain and Grief as Gateways

With living life from a place of love and eliminating the multitude of fear thoughts, lives will change. It is possible to experience a greater peace within. It is the Peace That Passes All Understanding. And along with these, of course, is Joy. Peace, Love and Joy! These are indeed gifts of the Spirit. How long I have known this, and yet, these were just words to me, albeit ones I spoke often. In the past, I had not experienced these gifts as I do now. Pain and grief can truly be gateways to our joy.

Recently, I found this poem channeled by Eva Pierrakos in her *Pathwork® Guide* Lecture 190.

Through the Gateway

Through the gateway of feeling your weakness,
lies your strength.
Through the gateway of feeling your pain,
lies your pleasure and joy.
Through the gateway of feeling your fear,
lies your security and safety.
Through the gateway of feeling your loneliness,
lies your capacity to have
fulfillment, love, and companionship.
Through the gateway of feeling your hate,
lies your capacity to love.
Through the gateway of feeling your hopelessness,
lies your true and justified hope.
Through accepting the lacks of your childhood,
lies your fulfillment now.

I have come through the gateway into a more joyous way of living. My journey of grief and fear of loss was difficult and extremely painful. It was the darkest time in my life. With the support of loving friends and family along with my faith, I began with baby steps to re-enter the world around me. From today's vantage point, I can clearly see how God was working in my life. Guidance moved with me through my grief and life started getting better.

Deep in my grief of three months, a very dear friend encouraged me to read author Sara Ban Breathnach's, *Simple Abundance* and *The Gratitude Journal*. Here I was guided to a wonderful tool. Each night before going to sleep I would write down at least five things I was grateful for that day. I began to keep a Gratitude Journal along with my regular journal. I believe by shifting my focus to one of gratitude for the blessings in my life, I started my journey to happiness and joy.

Just a few weeks into the Gratitude Journal, I started an archeological dig of my past to my inner self. This was a suggestion found in *Simple Abundance*. So I proceeded to go through boxes of things from my past, cleaning and clearing as I went. I knew this process was one way of getting rid of the old in order to make way for new things to enter my life. The surprise came when I discovered several old photos taken on my trip on the Domeline Zephyr from Nebraska to California. As a recent college graduate, I was on my way to begin my dietetic internship in Los Angeles.

In my journal I found the following entry. This came after asking Spirit's assistance.

Yes, there is much buried that we can recover and bring forth, perhaps a little at a time, so you can more fully appreciate each of the gems that are there within you. Do you remember how excited you were when you were heading to California in 1956 to start a new journey and adventure? You were leaving home and the familiar way of being. Going to a totally new place, yet undiscovered, the excitement was high and the adventure was fun for you. You were eager to be on with your life and experience being on your own. Well, this is now much like that time. You are heading into an unknown. Yes, it is different— you are in familiar surroundings, but the circumstances are very different. You need to remember the excitement and fun of the adventure into the great unknown. The changes are as vast for you now as they were then. The important thing for you to remember here is how full of courage and excitement you were to be moving on. This can be the same way if you let it. Feel the same excitement for the future. Approach living in this way being fully aware that it is an adventure and will bring you to a new place, a new life, a new way of being. Remember and bring these same feelings into your new adventure. You are in familiar surroundings but these also can be made new, fun, and exciting for you. People around you can and will change. It is going to be just as wonderful in this next part of your journey as it was then. You can go forth filled with the same kind of enthusiasm as you did in your total change of life at that juncture. Look again at the pictures you found from 1956. It was a pivotal time just as 1996 was a pivotal time. You began a new life for yourself and for this next portion it will be just as wonderful. Remember, know that you did it before and you can do it again. You have absolutely all you need to have within you.

This was certainly a gift from Spirit for my life began to take on a new perspective. As I recalled that time, I realized I could again find the courage I once had. Somehow, it had become covered up along the way. I found hope from these words that life could once again become an adventure. These were encouraging thoughts and they came at a time of great need. Just thinking that my life might be wonderful again gave me the courage and hope I had lost. I realized I had been here before.

My life did begin to change as I recalled my excitement of being on my own. If I was to believe the words that had been given to me, I needed to trust and believe my life would become just as full and exciting as it had 40 years before. That was a time of phenomenal growth for me. I had enjoyed my independence, making my own decisions. Maybe it would happen again.

Well, it certainly has been an adventure and I once again enjoy being independent. Growth is happening for me, this time in different ways. Now I frequently ask for guidance. When I take time to look back on all I have accomplished in the last couple of years, I know I have regained my courage. My friends and family affirm this.

Life is happier now and I have greater joy in living than I ever remember experiencing. This is not to say my life during my marriage and raising a family was unhappy. No, it was a wonderful time. I was truly blessed to have shared all those years with such a loving and caring man. In the years after the children were on their own, Don and I became extremely close and our relationship was wonderfully loving and happy.

Discovery of Shared Interests

Our interests in complimentary health care, healing, and holistic living were shared. This expanded as Don became interested in Reflexology. He attended several workshops and gained proficiency as a reflexologist throughout the last twelve years of his life. This is a unique avocation for one who was an engineer by profession. Certainly one of the benefits for me was his willingness to work on my feet on a fairly regular basis. Actually, I was one of his motivations in pursuing this since I seemed to have frequent needs, the biggest need being reducing the impact of menopause. We both found out about the benefits to be gained with this alternative treatment.

As in all things, one thing led to the next. When I decided to attend a Therapeutic Touch workshop about eight years later, Don wanted to attend, too. This is where we discovered another shared interest and learned about using the pendulum for dowsing. Our learning adventure was fun and led to more dowsing workshops. Being in the water business, Don became interested in locating water by dowsing. I discovered how well dowsing worked for me in determining which foods and supplements my body could tolerate. About the same time, we launched into a major remodeling of our home. We were delighted that with dowsing we could select the carpet which best coordinated with the five adjoining floor coverings. We had a lot of fun discovering all of these common interests.

It seemed as though we were finally at a point in our lives when we were enjoying life. We appreciated nature and liked being in our beautiful natural world. Don had grown up on a farm and being out in open spaces was appealing to him. I had lived in a city all of my childhood learning to appreciate our natural world from my Dad who had also been raised on a farm and enjoyed being outdoors. Dad taught me to listen to the sounds of nature— songs of the birds, wind in the trees, and rain drops falling.

Our walks were something Don and I looked forward to doing together. It was Don who decided this would be a good physical fitness activity for us. Initially, I resisted. My muscles would be hurting and I'd be out of breath as we went up the hills in our neighborhood. It wasn't hard to figure out who was most in need of exercise. As time went on, Don persisted in getting me to walk on a daily basis and it became easier. My fitness level improved considerably. Along with benefit to the body, it wasn't long before I recognized how much better everything functioned. My mind became clearer, anxiety or stress decreased, and I became energized. My body benefited physically, mentally, emotionally, and spiritually. In addition, the communication between us as we walked was better because of our giving full attention to what was being said. This enhanced our relationship. Walking and talking together became a time of mutual enjoyment.

While walking alone was difficult at first, it is now an anticipated activity— one that has become part of my regular routine. It is a time when I commune with nature and listen. Recently, Spirit came to me with a song. Words long forgotten formed on my lips, "Forget your troubles and just get happy." My entire being changed from concern to surprise to laughter and then to gratitude. It was a magical transformation from anxiety to joy. During this walk, I took a different route than my usual one and I saw how new everything looked. This was an opportunity for me to change perspectives. It was an "aha" moment.

Guidance from Within

Perspectives on many things are changing for me but also for others. Great change is taking place in the world creating a need to see with new eyes, to look within, and to open hearts. This time ahead necessitates knowing how to proceed and live life. It is my sense that those who are able to go within and connect with Spirit will find life easier and richer. It will be a more fulfilling and joyful time as life is really lived for the highest good. The way to greater happiness and joy in life is to trust communication with Spirit.

Practicing this communication makes it come easily. Like learning to play the piano, which starts slowly by discovering where the notes are on the keyboard, then step-by-step learning how to play the notes together. It is in the doing that the learning comes, and ultimately, the discovery of true pleasure and joy in creating music.

With anything unfamiliar, to a beginner it seems difficult. It is only by practicing what you don't know that it becomes easy. As it becomes easier, it becomes more fun. When learning to do it really well, pleasure is gained, and eventually, a more joyful experience is the result.

Seeking divine guidance from within is no different. When you begin to ask for information and help, you will find it is there. It has always been there, but until you become aware of this and seek to utilize it, it remains buried within. It is like a gemstone waiting to be uncovered and brought into life to be polished and utilized. Only then does it become the gift it is meant to be.

When living life utilizing this gift, I discovered how much easier life can be. Everything seems to fall into place as if there is an order to life. I step out of the chaos into an easier, more balanced way of living. I feel as though I am able to function at a higher level of being. A divine order or life plan is apparent to me. I am guided to take actions which bring harmony into my life. By living with greater harmony, I have found joy and the experience of more peace and love.

Vibrational Healing

Several years ago I became interested in vibrational healing, including aromatherapy. During the grieving process, my curiosity led me to learning more about essential oils, especially lavender essential oil (E.O.) with it's calming and soothing benefits of balancing and normalizing the mind and emotions. I discovered its additional effects of activating the immune system and relaxing the body. When experiencing agitation and stress in my life, I used lavender E.O. as a natural remedy rather than ingest medications.

My experimentation with essential oils was a bonus. In the early weeks when pain of my grief was so strong, I used Marjoram E.O. to lessen the intensity of the internal earthquakes. This enabled me to function better in my daily living. I have since discovered that Rose E.O. is perhaps a better choice when experiencing extreme bereavement and grief.

Another example of vibrational healing are the Bach Flower Essences. The Rescue Remedy of the Bach Flower Essences helped when I began to feel panic attacks. The essential oils and the Bach Flower Essences both assist in changing the vibrational level of our bodies. Knowing this, I continue to utilize this form of healing.

In the course of my exploration of essential oils, I learned that all spiritual traditions use fragrances because scent transports one to the realm of the divine. Instinctively, I began to use an aromatherapy candle with lavender E.O. during meditation. This proved to be calming to the senses, instilling a peace within. An entry in my journal was written after one of these meditations when I felt loved and blessed even though I didn't know what was ahead. Because I have faith in positive outcomes, I didn't need to know. I opened to God stating my trust that the future would unfold in good ways and that I would be guided to know the direction to follow. God responded.

Dear One, I am happy to be allowed to share this opportunity to be in direct communication with you. You have made great strides in the recent past. It is so good to see you in a happier and healthier state in mind, body, and spirit, more whole than you have been in the past. Continue to take care of you. Remember this is the time for you to rest, relax, and enjoy being who you are, to become fully in touch with the true essence of you, who you are and why you are here on the earth plane at this time. It is an exciting time. It is a time with a great deal of change. It is a time of new beginnings for you. Enjoy them, enjoy life, enjoy your family, those related and those who are part of you in other ways. You will begin to awaken in new ways, ways you have not known before. It is good. It is as it needs to be. Know how important you are in the process for many people. Many will look to you and see your incredible radiance and peace and will learn from you. There is nothing to fear. They will see that you have the faith and trust in life, in Spirit, in God, all that is. Let life flow through you to others, open to loving them fully. Those who will be in your path and come to you will benefit. Just know and trust this. You have learned and grown tremendously and will continue to grow and develop your special gifts to share with those who come to you seeking. Let your light shine and stay balanced. This is so very important and it will take conscious thought. It is very easy to lose one's sense of balance for there is a need to stay grounded and to continue to practice this, to meditate, to relax, to be at peace, to remain calm. Know you are loved beyond all you can imagine. There are many in spirit who are working with you and through you now. You need to be aware of this and allow it to happen. It is for good, yours and others around you.

And so it was. These were encouraging words for me coming at a time when I felt so vulnerable. Knowing the words were from Spirit and could be trusted eased my mind. Again, I had a lifeline. This along with dowsing, which verifies the messages received, has helped me to where I am now. I am in a much better place, one filled with so much more light than I have ever experienced before in my life.

Share the Love

With so many messages reminding me to open my heart and let the love flow to others, I have sought ways to do this. By focusing thoughts on others and consciously sending love is one way. It is important to take action, too. Giving hugs is one of my favorite ways. My hugs for others have always been gentle ones, sincerely given. These are the kind I most like receiving.

Thinking back it was my mother who introduced hugs to my family. She was a widow in her 70's and studying *A Course In Miracles* at the time. This study proved to be a transforming force in her life as she became more openly loving. It had a ripple effect in our family, including our teenage children.

At one point in our lives, Don and I decided to share this expression of our love for others. We began teaching a class at church on the healing ministry of Jesus called, "Luke on Wholeness." Since one of the ways Jesus healed was through touch, we talked about hugging being one of the ways we can be caring and supportive to others in a loving way. It is a form of touch with a healing intention. We became known as huggers and soon found many people seeking hugs on Sunday mornings. This delighted Don and seemed to bring much joy into his life as it still does to mine.

Listening is another way I show love to others. When actively listening to another person I give them my total attention. This is a rare thing in our world today. How often do you take the time to honor another human being in this way? To show them how much you care about what is happening in their life? Sometimes I think I need to solve their problem when all they really want is for me to listen and truly hear what is being said. Also, I am reminded to turn off my internal response while the other person is speaking so I can give my full attention to listening.

Living alone has brought this to my awareness in a new way. Although neither Don nor I really mastered this skill giving our complete attention to the other, there were opportunities to share our thoughts with one another. Now it is very different. It happens less frequently as family and friends are the ones I engage in conversation. Sharing intimate thoughts, those from the deepest place within, can be difficult to do except with a few trusted individuals. It seems easier for people to withdraw and not risk being vulnerable, unless they make an effort to reach out and open themselves.

Reaching out and letting myself be vulnerable are important steps. For me, it has meant opening myself and being willing to let others know me in new ways. In doing this, new opportunities have come to me as well as deeper relationships, some with people I have known much of my life. This is a joyful thing as we are brought together in our discovery of similar experiences of loss and grief. No longer do we exchange just common histories or interests, we reach for a more intimate sharing where our lives are enriched with life's purpose.

All in all, I am encouraged to be more open in sharing who I am with others and finding it well worth the risk. Through this process I am also learning more about who I am, the real Ruthie, the parts hidden from the world.

Chapter Four

Finding the Real Me

I awaken to Your Spirit within me, dear God, and see Your presence active in all creation.

Y ou become what you think is real. When you live year after year defining yourself by your role in life, you believe you are this role. You do not realize it could be any other way. This is what society and our culture support. Even though it was limiting, I became mere perceptions through a series of roles.

As circumstances changed, I assumed new roles and new identities. For instance, in this life I went from being a child to a student, to a dietitian, to a wife, to a mother, and now a widow. *But is this who I am?* It is certainly how I identified myself for many years. Not only was I a wife, but I was Don's wife. My identity was very much tied to my role and linked with my husband. The truth is I liked being his wife and would readily tell people that this was who I was.

Several years ago my self-definitions were shattered. Don, who had been company manager of the local office, decided to step down. No longer was I the manager's wife. This came as a big shock and I was forced to look at the reasons behind this. I discovered my identity had been tied up with pride. In other words, my ego sense of who I am reigned. Fortunately, at about the same time, I made conceptual discoveries through my spiritual work. One of these concepts was that I am not only my body. I am also spirit/soul/mind, one with the divine source, and I happen to have a body for this earthly experience.

This idea made sense to me as I believed in reincarnation, knowing I had lived many times before. However, integrating the concept and understanding it has not been easy. The ego identity continues to rear. After all, I am talking about a long term way of thinking. I remember one of my teachers saying we all have an inner *board of directors* — the many voices within us trying to be heard. Letting go of ego and freeing personal control is necessary, but is not easy to do. For a time, this would remain in my awareness and I would work on overcoming control, then life would present new challenges and the control issue would go to the back burner. I seemed to go back and forth remembering and forgetting, remembering and forgetting.

I found myself mostly forgetting and caught up in a myriad of activity. Of course, until the day I was without my beloved husband, then I was jolted with a reality I had not dreamed of having to face. This became a defining moment for me to either go forward living my life or be stuck in self-pity and great unhappiness.

Although difficult for a while, choosing to live has brought so many new opportunities into my life. Most importantly, the gift of time has been the opportunity for me to grow and develop in new ways. Having time to pursue my spiritual growth is one of the blessings. For many years, I tried to practice meditation early each morning. Sometimes this worked well, and at other times, setting aside 20 minutes for myself seemed impossible. Devotional reading and meditation became a life saver and making time for it now is a priority.

No longer an option, but a necessity, I choose to commune with the divine and with the spirit of my beloved husband. In these moments of silence, I receive messages of encouragement. I follow dialogues with Spirit by writing in my journal so the words can be read and reread. Spirit has long told me of my need to write so the words can be remembered, otherwise it is fleeting information and soon forgotten.

An Awakening

An opportunity unfolded step-by-step for me to travel to Arizona for a phenomenal experience with a spiritual healer. Everything fell into place quickly and easily as though it was being arranged. A friend extended an invitation for a nearby place to stay, my closest friend offered to travel with me, an appointment time was available when I wanted it, and the airline tickets were purchased at a discounted price. All the events seemed to be happening in divine order, moving me in one direction toward this healing.

During the healing, I experienced an incredible release of heavy dark feelings. Many issues were dealt with from early childhood to my recent loss. The bottom line though was the connection made with God, the love that is within. This was my awakening, I became aware of my authentic self. It has always been there within, yet I have looked for love to come from others. It was an awakening to find that I am a being of love. The incredible lightness felt in this healing process remains with me today.

Two days after this healing, I journaled a dialogue with my authentic self asking if there are choices I chose not to make and still feel the need to follow through and do.

Yes, there have been many choices you have made along the way. Each day holds many of these choices to be made. It would seem that you have at times made choices that appeared to you to be safe, not wanting to risk, perhaps being fearful of being who you are. This will be changing for you as you are beginning to be more in touch with that part of you that is your real self, your authentic self. I believe you will be surprised at how much fun you can have when you allow yourself to open up to the wonderful world and people that surround you. It will be a new and wonderful life for you.

Do not be concerned about what is in the past for it is the past. Live now in the present remembering that you are a new being and more in touch with the deep inner part of you than you have been for a very long time. It is an adventure you are just now embarking upon. Enjoy and experience the excitement of being an open and loving spirit. Ask and you will receive the answers. The choices will become very easy for you to make when you are following your inner guidance. It is there for the asking. Do not hesitate to use it. As you do this you will find that it will increase.

The knowing is within and you can learn much by utilizing this guidance. Live now, live with love and joy in your heart. You are filled with all that you need. It is a well that flows on continuously. This will include choices to be with people who are healthy and healing for you to be with, avoiding toxic people and places that can negate what you are about and what you are here to do. Continue on the path of awakening to your authentic self. It is a journey with great rewards.

Now, the journey within had greater focus with the intention to find the real self. My charge was to discover more about myself and how to live in this new awareness. As before, guidance was there for the asking. Although much of the help was of a personal nature and felt like it was coming from Don, there were times the guidance seemed to be general and broader in scope. After a time, I could sense the source of information and guidance.

I learned from Spirit while the love does come from within, it also comes from without. As I live with the love vibration flowing through me, I am reminded that living this way is the most important thing I can do for myself and others. It is especially important to remember the connection to God, the divine source. When all is going easily and well for me, I am aware of living in a love vibration. When living is an effort, it becomes necessary to stop and make the reconnection with the divine source for I have become separated.

Growing Myself

Timing is everything in this healing process. Soon after the healing, which had given me an inner connection with my divine nature, I began reading *Growing Myself*, a book by Judith Handelsman. It was early spring and soon it would be time to begin planting the annual flowers out doors. Having grown up with a father who always did the gardening and then a husband who also enjoyed working in the yard, I had come to believe this was not my job. Furthermore, I was not interested in getting my hands dirty. It wasn't that Don didn't try to interest and encourage me to work in the yard. He had. He knew how therapeutic it was to connect with nature. For me, my appreciation for nature came from observing, not doing.

A decision had to be made about the yard. If I was going to have flowers that I so enjoyed, it would either be up to me to garden or to find someone else to do it. Because of the way the words in *Growing Myself* captivated me, I decided to give gardening a try. The book is a spiritual journey through gardening which reflected my process where I was literally growing myself. In the beginning, I certainly did not know what I was doing. But answers were soon found to my questions and guided me through this learning process. I went within and asked for the help I was seeking and the answers came. I could feel Don's presence encouraging me along the way. On occasion, I would find myself laughing out loud as discoveries were made, like lawn mowing, which was a totally new experience for me.

Being in the solitude of a flower garden and digging in the soil has become more like play than work. Often this activity has brought me into conversations with a neighbor who has long known the benefits of gardening. There is so much I am learning from her about plants and their care. We have become more acquainted and appreciate the gifts we have to share, one of the many benefits gardening has provided. Nurturing my garden and my soul is a continuous process in growth. We are works in progress.

Working with plants, whether outside or inside the house, has shown me about the interconnectedness of all of life. Plants respond to the love I give them in much the same way people do. Either they flourish and grow to become all they can be, or wilt and wither, if loving care and nurture is withdrawn. Plants are teachers and have taught me about life when I am open to receive their messages. In that, my heart fills with gratitude for the things they have offered me in my journey of discovery.

It is a discovery process uncovering the layers of protection so carefully put in place by ourselves through the years. The layers become much like a steel armor held firmly in place and not easily removed until the day something breaks through. For me, it was through the skillful and persistent removal by a healer who brought me face-to-face with the emotional experiences that had caused the armor to be put in place. By releasing the tears and pain, I was assisted in dissolving the armor and allowing light to fill the space. This was a beginning and the process continues one step at a time.

In hindsight, it is easy to see the progressive steps of my journey, far easier than it was while going through them. It has been an orderly unfoldment. I asked to grow, to become healed and whole, and balanced in body, mind, and spirit. This was initiated through meditation and journaling, yet at the same time Spirit was guiding me in quiet and gentle ways. It took the periods of solitude to allow Spirit the opportunity of reaching me. Spirit guided me to the information for my healing, the understanding of who I am, and the clarity of my purpose.

Finding New Meaning in the Old

Words in books I had read previously took on new meaning. Only three months before Don's transition, a spiritual counselor suggested I read *Letters of the Scattered Brotherhood* by Mary Strong published in 1948. Amazingly, there was one lone copy on a book table at the annual conference of SFFI. I bought it and began using it as my daily devotional reading. In retrospect, I feel this was Spirit's way of preparing me for the time just ahead. On the book cover, I read:

The kingdom of heaven is happiness because those who have found it and abide in it have become aware of the beauty of the infinite Spirit. Those who live in that kingdom know that everything must be met and challenged with a shout; challenge everything with the Spirit of joy. This may seem a hard saying for it seems to leave out pity. No, the lifting quality of confidence, of faith in ultimate victory, heals, sustains, and comforts those in darkness and sorrow. The secret is— and this is what you are here for— to find the pearl of great price, to keep from losing it, from letting it grow dull and to remember that it has the power to release you from those characteristics which have held you a prisoner in your own limitations. This is being on the side of the angels.

What I understood when I first read the book and what the meaning holds for me now are completely different. *The secret is— and this is what you are here for …the power to release you from those characteristics which have held you a prisoner in your own limitations* jumps off the page. This is exactly what I had been doing, limiting myself, the real me, from recognizing who I really am. When I reflect on the process of these last three years, I am in awe of how wondrous and magical life really is when I step out of the way and allow the divine within to guide me.

Trusting and allowing are the necessary keys to this process. Trust loosens control. When I can release my need to control and allow my divine inner Spirit to guide me, I begin to live a very different life. This means letting go of my ego or that part of me wanting to maintain control. It is not an easy thing to do. In the past, I maintained a comfort level by staying in control. This is the way I had been taught to function by the world around me. This is the way many have been taught in the past.

There is an opportunity of learning new ways of living and new ways of being. You may be realizing an emptiness within yourself and are seeking greater happiness and fulfillment. The ways of living in our world often require being with things in the outer world. There has been a constant striving for acquisition, to make more money, and to buy more things. A hunger within longs to be satisfied so you attempt to buy happiness. After one desire is obtained, the search and longing continues, because you are still not completely happy and satisfied. Your true heart's desire has not been fulfilled, something is still missing.

The quiet longing within is still there. *Is it because you have not taken the time to find out who you really are, your real self?* More and more this has become apparent to me. What really matters is the connection with source, with the divine Spirit, with God. One very dark and rainy day when the news in the world was particularly unsettling, I asked Spirit for guidance.

Bring joy to yourself, to your being, let the light in. Let it build within and without. Be conscious of this. Be conscious of allowing yourself to be in the present moment. Savor each moment for the joy in it. The joy of life, of breath, of love, of peace and the joy of living life fully and completely. This is a time to be with yourself and find joy and happiness in this. Know you are loved, receive this love, and pass it on.

A significant shift occurred in my being after receiving this. When I am reminded to be in the present moment, to experience the light and love within and around me, I remember the essence of who I am. At the core of my being I am Spirit, you are Spirit, all are Spirit, and we are interconnected. Remembering this brings me to a new and different level of being. What I do and how I act does have an effect on others. This is a part of the interconnectedness of all things. Knowing this begins to have an impact on how life is lived. If I live my life with greater joy, others will begin to recognize this and possibly begin to believe they can experience greater joy in living, too.

Allowing

Just now as I write about experiencing joy, a hummingbird is visiting a tiny flower on my deck. In my symbols book, hummingbirds represent the absolute energy and joy in delving into the nectar of life. Since they fly upwards, downwards, and even backwards, they are reminding us to expand our joyous energy in all directions. I find the synchronicity of this quite fascinating. This beautiful little creature brings great joy to me and I am again in awe of the majesty and mystery of it all.

At almost the same moment outside my window, a single strand of a spider's web catches my eye as it sparkles in the sunlight. There is amazing strength and beauty in this tiny filament as it holds a leaf from a mighty oak tree. The other leaves in the cluster are fluttering in the breeze, but not this one.

It stands straight out from the rest attached to a web several feet away by this single tiny thread in a horizontal line. *How could such a small creature accomplish this feat?* Such is the wonder of this intricate system in nature.

It is absolutely amazing to behold the miracle of creation in our natural world. I so often lost sight of these wonders in much the same way I lost sight of myself, a miraculous creation. Each one of us is so unique, yet all of us are created in the image of God. The divine is in us, through us, and all around us. How can we not be awed by this mystery of life?

Human beings are miracles. We come into this world filled with joy, giving expression with radiant smiles as a baby and peals of laughter as a toddler. Watch a baby making new discoveries or a toddler at play to see the joy and delight coming from them. But all too soon this spontaneity in expressing delight in simply being is lost. Somewhere along the way we seem to close down and disconnect from this great joy in living.

Now is the time to begin reversing this process and start finding that joy again. When our natural state is fully realized, life changes. We are connected to an eternal Spirit, one with God. There is no separation from God because we carry that divine spark within. It is the light of being. It is our essence. Each human being carries a uniqueness that no one can match— an individuality to be celebrated—and at the same time, is connected by this divine essence as brothers and sisters in our global family.

The following are helpful words about the Inner Experience of connecting with the holy Spirit from *The Journey With The Master* by Eva Bell Werber:

Often when my children try to make their contact with me, they make effort; they labor and strive over what is so simple a thing; they think there should be an outer manifestation. In their thinking some great light should appear, some shining figure should stand before them, or they should have a queer bodily sensation. I declare to you this is not true. As you contact me, your holy Spirit within, it is an inner experience to be met on the plane of the Soul consciousness. It is so necessary that the joy of the union of Soul and Spirit, with the consequent knowledge of oneness, be made on this, the highest of all planes. It cannot take place otherwise.

It is necessary to lay aside emotional senses along with perceptions and desires by raising consciousness to the level of no emotion, except for that deep inner abiding oneness with the Presence. The power received from this close communion awakens the senses to the beauty and joy in the outer world. Even though this may seem like only a time of quiet peaceful resting, experiences can manifest in the world in unimaginable ways, such that one moment of joy transforms a world of negativity. The key is allowing ourselves to spend time in this manner.

Short periods of time with the Presence scattered through out the day help me to function at a higher level of being. These serve to remind me of my true self and my connection to Spirit.

In this way, I am able to practice the Presence, feeling more connected and whole, throughout my day. Somehow it is easier knowing I can go within, make the connection, and peacefully rest in this place if only for five or ten minutes at a time. The benefits from this practice reinforce my desire for continuing it.

With the passing of time and with a deep desire to let myself grow into the person I am meant to become, I find I am more in tune with spirit and guidance. It is becoming easier to be real. Being real means opening up and allowing others to see and get to know me just as I am without pretense or facade. It means risking and being vulnerable in order to become authentic and true to my self. Becoming real is one of my goals.

Chapter Five

Knowing Love Never Ends

For in love, there is no separation.

Through these months which have grown into years since that day when my life changed, I have experienced so much. Opportunities have come, enriching my life and bringing great joy. One of the most joyful is the birth of my first grandchild. Watching a baby grow and develop and experiencing the love which comes with this is unparalleled in my life. Yes, I experienced this before with my own children, yet this time it is different as any grandparent knows. This time I am free to just enjoy this "circle of love," the giving and receiving of pure unconditional love.

My ability to give and receive a stronger and deeper love is expanding. With intentional work through a variety of healing modalities, I am allowing further opening of my heart beyond the initial awakening. Slowly the missing pieces are found and fitting together. Following another profound spiritual healing, my healer asked me to write down *The Ways I Honor and Please Myself.* I was stumped. Initially, nothing came to my mind, but then slowly after a little conversation and prompting, I began to write.

1. By knowing what is my issue versus what is someone else's issue.
2. By creating a beautiful and peaceful place for myself, including my office/work space.
3. By hugging those I love.
4. By taking care of my physical body through frequent exercise and eating healthy foods.
5. By being with the people I enjoy.
6. By having fresh flowers in the house.
7. By listening to my inner guidance.
8. By dowsing.
9. By listening to my body and resting when needed.
10. By allowing myself to take time to just "be."
11. By having fun and laughing.

My healer encouraged me to continue adding to this list because other ways I honor myself would come to mind. This query gave me the realization of the ways I can and do demonstrate love for myself. My memories include many incidents of self-judgment where I overlooked honoring and celebrating myself. I could condemn myself for this but I prefer to remember and celebrate the being I am, honoring and loving myself.

For, I believe, in honoring and loving ourselves unconditionally, we are able to give unconditional love to others. Loving ourselves without judgment is a necessary beginning. Once we come to this place, passing on unconditional love to others in our life becomes easier. It requires letting go of condemning ourselves and others.

Balance All Things

With unconditional love, there are no expectations, petitions, or strings attached. It is an acceptance of being loved as we are right now, the way we are loved by God. I believe love is an energy vibration and is "felt" by us. I am often reminded by Spirit in my journaling communications to open myself to receive the love that is being sent to me, to feel it, and know it is there for me. Believing this to be true and acknowledging this flow of love energy seem to be key in allowing it to enter my being. When I do these things, it seems I can actually perceive love coming to me. This perception has been amplified by my awareness of times when I have blocked and closed off these vibrations. Those are specific times when I am hurt, angry, depressed, fearful, or feeling the pain of loss. These times reveal that I am not centered or in balance.

A message I have frequently received is to stay in balance. For quite a while this caused considerable consternation, trying to figure out what this meant. *What does it mean to be in balance? What am I to balance in my life?* One day this was part of a long message.

Let your light shine. Stay balanced. This is so very important and it will take conscious thought. It is very easy to lose one's sense of balance. You need to stay grounded and to continue to practice this, to meditate, to relax, to be at peace, to remain calm....

Another day the message was:

Perhaps it might be helpful to schedule some time for writing and some time for exercising, etc. Balance it in whatever way feels right to you. You are aware that it is good to vary the activity, quiet and active. Keep things in balance. One will help the other.

This was clearly stated and good advice. Like establishing a balance between work and play, it meant spending time in quiet and also in activity. I understood this one. Then a month later I received further guidance.

You are aware of the need for balance so build it into your life in all things.

Oh my, this felt like a tall order to balance "all things." Was this indicating my need to keep a sense of equilibrium between opposites and not be drawn into issues around me? I find this easier said than done. However, the importance of doing this has not eluded me.

Then several months later, following some work in letting go of "old baggage" and beginning to feel a transforming lightness in my body, another message about balance came.

Yes, it is important to maintain your balance through this and continue to stay centered and well-grounded.

One day I was feeling some anxiety about attending an event where I would be with many people holding opposing views, I sat down to dialogue with Don in my journal. Don was very helpful.

Know that your presence will be most helpful to all when you are in a balanced state and expressing love. All are needing the love vibration. You know how to let this flow through you and this will be helpful to the atmosphere and climate of the space. So as you can detach yourself from involvement at a personal or egoic level try to bring this love presence, light, into the room. Send love to each as you sit in the room, remain detached and stay in your center. Know you are surrounded by many angelic beings and those in spirit. The way of love is the way. Be at one with Spirit and if pulled away from this you can bring yourself back into the centered place. You can do this and this is all you really need to do. You will not be called on to say anything, but your presence radiating light and love to all is needed. The great calming influence you bring just with your being there. This is the gift you bring.

After thanking Don for this message, I felt much more at peace and moved to try my hand at poetry. I asked Spirit to bring forth what might be of help for me at this time.

Live in the light. Be a light to all.
You are the one who does know how.
It's up to you to show the way
the way of love straight from the heart.
So open up and let it flow

From up above, on out through you
to all who now know fear of change.
The love, you see, dissolves the fear
and brings a sense of peaceful calm
to all who need this greater light.
From heart to heart the love will flow
dissolving fear from pain filled hearts.

Love Letters

These messages provided a focus for loving others without judgment and remaining in a centered and balanced state. Love is the overriding message in the communications I have received. For me, they are love letters reminding me of how much I am loved, of the importance of receiving and giving love, and of letting others know they are loved.

The following "love letter" is among the earliest ones I received while writing in my journal about how much I was missing my husband and feeling the pain of my loss.

Please my dear, let me have a turn at this. I do love you so much. Nothing has or ever will change that. You are my true love and always will be. I am constantly sending you that message. Yes, it has to be hard for you, especially now, and it is hard for me to see you feeling sad. But know that it is very good to let the tears flow as you are now. It will help you with your physical body. The sinuses are full and are needing the release as are your nerves and emotional self.... Know this is a time for you to rest for a while now. Slow down and spend time just relaxing and enjoying being, regenerate yourself. If you don't do this, it will be damaging to your health. I really need to have your attention to this. Rest, relax, enjoy just doing nothing part of the day. Read something entertaining, laughter would be good for you.… Remember to be aware of what your body is saying to you. Thank you for this time to be able to give a little guidance to you. I am here to help you through this, so please let me help you. I love you!

A few months later Don expanded his love message to me. This one followed my healing session in Arizona and came after I had returned home. He expressed his happiness at my improved state of being.

It is so good to see you experiencing so much more joy in your life. That is so important for you, for your health, and your well being. You will notice that your body will be in better and better condition as time goes on.… We will continue to be working together and things will be good. Know it and trust it. Remember I love you and am sending you my love energy along with that of many others. Yes, the love comes from within you, but it also does come from without. You are very aware when you are in a love vibration. All goes smoothly and feels good. Thank you for your love and support. It is important to me as well. Remember to live with the love vibration flowing from you in all that you do. It is the most important thing you can do for yourself and all others. Yes, send your love out to all in the family. All are in need of this and they will know and will respond accordingly. Continue now to take care of you and keep this love growing in you and flowing from you. Have fun! Remember to play and laugh and dance to your hearts content. Lighten up and live fully my dear.

A Voice of the Eternal

In addition to the many written messages, I received a number of them by hearing a voice shortly before 6 A.M. Each time I was awakened by this voice I wondered who was there in my bedroom talking to me. The messages came within the first six or seven months of Don's passing with specific instructions to write them down so I would not forget.

Be happy my dear. Live in love. Love yourself. Love others. This is most important!

Wonderfully good advice I was obviously not yet practicing at that time.

Relax, let me help you, hang loose.

This one woke me up and I laid in bed asking, "Help me with what?" The sense that came was to help me with everything. Later, dowsing confirmed this.

Live in Peace, Love and Joy!

I seemed to keep getting this message. One day at a conference, I mentioned this to a college age girl who quickly told me, "Until you start doing this, you will keep getting the message." How true this is!

I love you for always, I love you completely, I love you forever.

This message I now believe completely for love is eternal. There is no ending point, not even with death.

One message was quite different. I was awakened by a voice saying,

You were shot in the heart in October.

This one was quite unsettling. It was not until I was fully awake did I realize that it was October when Don suddenly left me and went into spirit. I did indeed feel like being shot in my heart. There have been other messages during early morning hours before awakening, but they are far less frequent these days. Perhaps I am now more able to recognize these messages intuitively or by ESP throughout the day. I am learning to open myself more fully and regularly to that voice.

I am really grateful to have written these messages. The advantages to having it recorded on paper came in the following message at the end of several pages.

When I can put it on paper then I know you are getting my message and can read it over again and each time you do you will begin to believe it and know it is true. True— this is true. Life is for living and loving and being filled with Joy. Do not forget that. This is the most important message I can give you. Trust that when you can live it, others will get the message as well by observing you. I love you my dear.

Sweet Mystery

Recently, I found myself singing the first line of a song, written long before I was born. It comes from a 1910 operetta *Naughty Marietta* by Victor Herbert. I remembered hearing this song in my youth, but did not know the words beyond the first line. I felt compelled to search for these words and to share them as this seemed to be another of the gifts from Spirit. My kids tell me that the song is featured in a Mel Brooks movie, but my association predates Madeline Kahn.

Ah! Sweet mystery of life, at last I've found thee;
Ah! I know at last the secret of it all;
All the longing, striving, seeking, waiting, yearning,
The burning hopes, the joys, and idle tears that fall!
For 'tis love, and love alone, the world is seeking;
And it's love, and love alone, that can repay;
'Tis the answer, 'tis the end and all of living,
For it is love alone that rules for aye!

And so it is! Living life fully with great joy in my heart and sharing my love are my goals. Keeping the circle alive by giving and receiving, giving and receiving, giving and receiving. The circle of love knows no end.

Books That Have Influenced My Journey

Altea, Rosemary, *The Eagle and The Rose*, New York: Warner Books, 1996.

_____, *Proud Spirit*, New York: Eagle Brook Morrow, 1997.

_____, *You Own The Power*, New York: Eagle Brook Morrow, 2000.

Althouse, Lawrence W., *Rediscovering the Gift of Healing*, York Beach, ME: Samuel Weiser, 1983 (originally published by Abingdon Press, 1977).

Atwater, P.M.H., *Coming Back To Life: The After-Effects Of The Near-Death Experience*, New York: Bantam Books, 1988.

Bethards, Betty, *The Dream Book, Symbols for Self-Understanding*, Petaluma, CA: Inner Light Foundation, 1983.

Brennan, Barbara Ann, *Hands Of Light: A Guide to Healing Through the Human Energy Field*, New York: Bantam Books, 1987.

Borysenko, Joan, Ph.D., *Minding The Body, Mending The Mind*, New York: Bantam, 1987.

_____, and Miroslav Borysenko, *The Power Of The Mind To Heal: Renewing Body, Mind and Spirit*, Carson, CA: Hay House, 1994.

Ban Breathnach, Sara, *Simple Abundance*, New York: Warner Books, 1995.

Brinkley, Dannion with Paul Perry, *Saved By the Light*, Wheeler Publishing, 1994.

Bruyere, Rosalyn L., *Wheels of Light: A Study of the Chakras* Volume 1, Arcadia, CA: Bon Productions, 1989.

Cameron, Julia with Mark Bryan, *The Artist's Way: A Spiritual Path to Higher Creativity*, New York: Tarcher/Putnam, 1992.

Clark, Glenn, *The Man Who Tapped the Secrets of the Universe*, Swannanoa, Waynesboro, VA: The University of Science and Philosophy, 1946.

Course in Miracles, Foundation for Inner Peace, 1975

Delbene, Ron with Herb Montgomery, *The Hunger of the Heart*, Winston Press, 1983.

Eadie, Betty J., *Embraced By The Light*, Placerville, CA: Gold Leaf Press, 1992.

Exupery, Antoine de Saint, *The Little Prince*, New York: Harcourt, Brace and World, 1971.

Foster, Richard J., *Freedom of Simplicity*, San Francisco, CA: Harper, 1998.

_____, *Celebration of Discipline: The Path to Spiritual Growth*, San Francisco, CA: Harper & Row, Revised Edition, 1988.

_____, *Prayer: Finding the Hearts True Home*, San Francisco, CA: Harper Collins, 1992.

Gas, Robert with Kathleen Brehony, *Chanting: Discovering Spirit In Sound*, New York: Broadway Books, 1999.

Gawain, Shakti, *Creative Visualization*, San Rafael, CA: New World Library, 1978.

_____, *Living In the Light: A Guide to Personal and Planetary Transformation*, San Rafael, CA: New World Library, 1986.

_____, *The Path Of Transformation: How Healing Ourselves Can Change The World*, Mill Valley, CA: Nataraj Publishing, 1993.

Gaynor, Mitchell, M.D., *Sounds of Healing: A Physician Reveals the Therapeutic Power of Sound, Voice and Music*, New York: Broadway Press,1999.

Gerber, Richard, M.D., *Vibrational Medicine: New Choices For Healing Ourselves*, Santa Fe, NM: Bear and Company, 1988.

_____,. *Vibrational Medicine For the 21st Century: The Complete Guide to Energy Healing and Spiritual Transformation*, New York: Harper Collins, 2000.

Gibran, Kahlil, *The Prophet*, New York: Alfred A. Knopf, Inc., 1951.

Gimbel, Theo, *Healing With Color And Light*, New York: Fireside Book by Simon & Schuster, 1994.

Greaves, Helen, *Testimony Of Light*, Marina del Rey, CA: DeVorss, 1989.

Green, Glenda, *Love Without End: Jesus Speaks*, Fort Worth, TX: Heartwings Publishing, 1999.

Goldsmith, Joel S., *The Art Of Meditation*, New York: Harper & Row, 1956.

Grollman, Earl A., *Living When A Loved One Has Died*, Boston, MA: Beacon Press, 1977.

Grosjean, Nelly, *Aromatherapy: Essential Oils for Your Health*, Marseille, France.

Guggenheim, Bill and Judy Guggenheim, *Hello From Heaven*, New York: Bantam Books, 1996.

Handelsman, Judith, *Growing Myself: A Spiritual Journey Through Gardening*, New York: Dutton, 1996.

Hay, Louise L., *You Can Heal Your Life*, Santa Monica, CA: Hay House, 1984.

Helleberg, Marilyn Morgan, *Beyond TM: A Practical Guide to the Lost Traditions of Christian Meditation*, New York: Paulist Press, 1980.

Jampolsky, Gerald G., M.D., *Love Is Letting Go Of Fear*, Millbrae, CA: Celestial Arts, 1979.

_____, *Teach Only Love*, New York: Bantam Books, 1983.

_____, *Goodbye to Guilt*, New York: Bantam Books, 1985.

Joy, W. Brugh, M.D., *Joy's Way: A Map for the Transformational Journey*, CA: J.P. Tarcher, Inc. 1979.

Kelsey, Morton T., *Caring: How Can We Love One Another?*, Ramsey, NJ: Paulist Press, 1981.

Keys, Ken, Jr., *The Hundreth Monkey*, St. Mary, KY: Vision Books, 1982.

Krieger, Dolores, *Accepting Your Power to Heal: The Personal Practice of Therapeutic Touch*, Santa Fe, NM: Bear and Company, 1993.

Kubler - Ross, Elisabeth, M.D., *On Death and Dying*, New York: Macmillan, 1969.

_____, *Death the Final Stage of Growth*, Englewood Cliffs, NJ: Prentice Hall, 1975.

_____, *On Life After Death*, Berkeley, CA: Celestial Arts, 1991.

Lerner, Harriet, PhD, *The Dance of Anger*, New York: Harper & Row, 1985.

LeSan, Lawrence, *How To Meditate*, Boston, MA: Little Brown & Company, 1974.

Lindbergh, Anne Morrow, *Gift from the Sea*, New York: Vintage Books (Random House), 1955.

Linn, Denise, *The Secret Language of Signs*, New York: Ballantine Books, 1996.

Lunny, Vivian, M.D., *Aromatherapy: The Complete Guide to Aromatherapy for Natural Healing, Relaxation and Beauty*, London, England: Smithmark Publishers, 1997.

MacLaine, Shirley, *Out On A Limb*, New York: Bantam Books, 1983.

Mandino, Og, *The Greatest Secret In the World*, New York: Bantam Books, 1972.

Milanovich, Dr. Norma and Dr. Shirley McCune, *The Light Shall Set Your Free*, Albuquerque, NM: Athena Publishing, 1996.

Montgomery, Ruth, *A Search for the Truth*, New York: Bantam Books, 1967.

_____, *A World Beyond*, New York: Fawcett Crest Books, 1971.

Moody, Raymond A. Jr. M.D., *Life After Life*, New York: Bantam Books, 1975.

_____, *The Light Beyond*, New York: Bantam Books, 1988.

Morse, Melvin, M.D. with Paul Perry, *Parting Visions: Uses and Meanings of Pre Death, Psychic and Spiritual Experiences*, New York: Villard Books, 1994.

Parker, William R. and Elaine St. Johns, *Prayer Can Change Your Life*, Paramus, NJ: 1957 (out of print).

Peck, M. Scott, *The Road Less Traveled*, New York, NY, Simon and Schuster, 1980.

Progoff, Ira, *The Basic Text and Guide for Using the Intensive Journal Process*, New York: Dialogue House, 1975.

_____, *The Practice of Process Meditation: The Intensive Journal Way to Spiritual Experience*, New York: Dialogue House, 1980.

Puryear, Anne, *Stephen Lives*, Pocket Books, 1992.

Redfield, James, *The Celestine Prophecy*, New York: Warner Books, 1993.

_____, *The Secret Of Shambhala*, New York: Warner Books, 1999.

Ritchie, George G. Jr. with Elizabeth Sherrill, *Return From Tomorrow*, New York: Fleming H. Revell Company, 1978.

Ross, T. E. and Richard D. Wright, *The Divining Mind: A Guide to Dowsing and Self Awareness,* Rochester, VT, Destiny Books, 1990.

Sanford, Agnes, *The Healing Gifts of the Spirit,* J.B. Lippincott Company, 1966.

Trine, Ralph Waldo, *In Tune With The Infinite,* Indianapolis, New York: The Bobs Merrill Company, Inc, 1970 (1908 original copyright).

Seigel, Bernie S., M.D., *Love, Medicine and Miracles,* New York: Harper & Row, 1986.

_____, *Peace, Love and Healing: Bodymind Communication and the Path to Self-Healing: An Exploration,* New York, Harper and Row, 1987.

Shinn, Florence Scovel, *The Game of Life and How to Play It,* Marina del Rey, CA, DeVorss & Company, 1988.

Simonton, O. Carl, M.D. and Stephanie Matthews-Simonton, *Getting Well Again,* New York: Bantam Books, 1978.

Steadman, Alice, *Who's The Matter With Me?,* Marina del Rey, CA, DeVorss and Co., 1981.

Stein, Diane, *Essential Reiki: A Complete Guide To An Ancient Healing Art,* Freedom, CA: The Crossing Press, Inc., 1995.

Strong, Mary, *Letters of the Scattered Brotherhood,* New York, Harper & Row, 1948.

Tisserand, Maggie, *Aromatherapy For Women: A Practical Guide to Essential Oils for Health and Beauty,* Rochester, VT: Healing Arts Press, 1985.

Truman, Karol K., *Feelings Buried Alive Never Die*, Las Vegas, NV: Olympus Distributing, 1991.

Van Praagh, James, *Talking To Heaven: A Medium's Message of Life After Death*, New York: Dutton Press, 1997.

_____, *Reaching To Heaven: A Spiritual Journey Through Life and Death*, New York: Dutton Press, 1999.

Weiss, Brian L., M.D., *Many Lives, Many Masters*, New York: Simon & Schuster, 1988.

_____, *Messages From the Masters: Tapping Into The Power Of Love*, New York: Warner Books, 2000.

Werber, Eva Bell, *In His Presence*, Marina del Rey, CA: DeVorss & Company, Sixth Printing 1985 (copyright 1946).

_____, *The Journey With The Master*, Marina del Rey, CA: DeVorss & Company, Seventeenth Printing 1990 (copyright 1950).

Whitton, Joel, M.D., PhD, *Life Between Life*, New York: Warner Books, 1986.

Williamson, Marianne, *A Return To Love*, New York: HarperCollins Publishers, 1992.

Yogananda, Paramahansa, *Autobiography of a Yogi*, Los Angeles, CA: Self Realization Fellowship Publishers, 1973.

Zi, Nancy, *The Art Of Breathing*, New York: Bantam Books, 1986.

Zukhav, Gary, *The Seat of the Soul*, New York: Simon and Schuster, 1990.

Postscript

Several months after the attack on the World Trade Center, my friends Joy and Marv Johnson were telling of their grief counseling work in New York and New Jersey with some of those closely affected. A comment Joy made in her presentation struck me as important to pass on to others: *When we tell our story, we begin our healing.* I again realized how much the process of writing and telling my story helped me move through my grief into a place where I feel more joy in living. It has been a big part of my healing journey — healing is a continuing process.

The passage of time has also played a part. I can truly say I have moved through grief to joy and this feels very good. I am still profoundly affected by his passing and have waves of emotion, wishing Don was with me in body. The moments are farther apart now.

We celebrated my mother's 100th birthday with great joy almost 6 years after Don's transition. That same year my second grandchild was born. This was another joyful celebration for me and my family. Watching my two grandchildren grow brings me great joy. I know his presence is with us and he is loving every moment.

At a workshop I remember hearing: *When we make our transition to spirit, the only thing we will be asked is... Did you dance with your passion? Did you play with your joy?* This reinforces my feeling of the importance of living life with joy in my heart. I focus more now on dancing with my passion and playing with my joy. These are my goals—dancing and playing—helping me to "lighten up".

With Deep Gratitude

My love and deepest gratitude to my husband Don for his continuing love and support. Also to my family who supported me through my grief while they were dealing with their own grief process. To my daughter, Julie, my son, Jeff, and to my mother, Frances Ernst who depended on Don as father, son in law, trusted advisor and loving supporter, my deepest love and gratitude.

Blessings to Alice Rushton and Twink Dalton whose immediate support helped me through that first night and the following days along with my pastor, Jimmy Creech. Special thanks to our closest friends, Dick and Dorothy Heckman, for taking me to our townhouse at Holiday Island, AR two weeks later. Thanks to my friends and extended family too numerous to list -- you know who you are. Your support and love was there when I needed it.

To my editor and dear friend, Lynette Marie Hanthorn, who by using her many gifts made my words flow smoothly with magical transitions, I am deeply indebted. Her support throughout the process of writing helped my healing more than I realized at the time.

Thank you, SFFI board members Sandra Nohre, Judith McLean, Marvin Witbeck and Elizabeth "Pat" Fenske.

To my reviewers, Loyie Weber, Coco Chapman, Madonna Braun, Joy Johnson, Sandra Nohre and Seanne Emerton, your suggestions and comments were greatly appreciated.

Finally to Marlene Lomax and Diane Hansen, thank you for your encouragement to actually publish this book.

Julie, Jeff and Ben, thanks for the technical support!

Permissions

Sara Ban Breathnach, *Simple Abundance*, New York: Warner Books, 1995

Denise Linn, *The Secret Language of Signs*, New York, Random House, 1996

DeVorss Publications, Marina del Rey, California for use of *Journey With The Master* by Eva Bell Werber (copyright 1950)

Quotation from The Pathwork Guide Lecture Material (copyright 2000) The Pathwork Foundation. Reprinted by permission of the Pathwork Foundation. For use of Through the Gateway channeled by Eva Pierrakos in Pathwork Guide Lecture 190.

About the Author

Ruthie practices holistic health, is an experienced dowser using her pendulum and does energy healing techniques of Therapeutic Touch and Reiki. Ruthie has lived in Omaha, Nebraska for more than fifty years.